Old Bubbies Club
ADOPTION DAY!

Copyright © 2021 by Mary Maxey-Rodgers

Illustrations by Satria Lemburusa

It's adoption day at Old Timer Rescue! Tails are wagging, and excited howling can be heard throughout the center as senior pups—dogs that are over the age of 7—await meeting their future families.

Sisters Gladys (age 8, tan chihuahua-pug), Phyllis (age 9, black chihuahua), and Trudy (age 10, black and brown miniature pincher) sat in their beds, happily smiling as families walk by.

"Maybe today is the day!" said happy-go-lucky Trudy.
"I'm not so sure. People make me nervous," said Phyllis.
"We've been here a long time," exclaimed Gladys. "But I have a good feeling about today!"

The hours pass by, but none of the girls get adopted. "I told you," said Phyllis. "Don't get your hopes up."
"But everyone else got adopted...it will have to be our turn soon," Trudy positively stated.
"One day...when it's our turn....we'll go to our forever home," replied Gladys.

Meanwhile, about an hour away in a cozy house on Cowboy Lane, a small family was going through a hard time. The Chavez family lost Mr. Chavez when he died the year prior, and only Mrs. Chavez and little Henry remained. Mother and young son felt sad and lost.

Mrs. Chavez and little Henry continued going to work and to school, but something was missing. They missed Mr. Chavez, and the house was just too quiet.

Henry arrived at school one day to learn that there will be a special assembly at lunch. Old Timer Rescue will be coming to their school to let the children meet their senior dogs and show them what good pets seniors can be.

The Old Timer Rescue presenters talked about how often no one wants to adopt a senior dog. People are afraid that they are too old and won't be fun pets. They spoke about how senior dogs end up in shelters and don't get to be with a family that loves them.

There were so many great senior dogs, and they were playful and cute. Henry couldn't stop thinking about them. Suddenly he had a great idea!

Henry had never had a dog before, but he's excited to tell his mom about the dogs he met. Running home from school, he burst through the door and yelled to his mom, "MOM! MOM! I HAVE THE BEST IDEA! Let's adopt a dog! And not just any dog...a SENIOR DOG!"

Later, that evening, Henry told his mom about all the great dogs he had met that day. He shared how sad it was that just because they were older, they didn't have a family. People didn't want older dogs, and it didn't seem fair. "Can we get a senior dog, Mom?" Henry asked, wild-eyed.

Mrs. Chavez smiled. She hadn't seen Henry this excited and happy in a long time. "Let me think about it, okay, Henry?"

Henry is too excited to sleep. He wondered if he will really get a dog. He finally drifted off to sleep and dreams of running through a park and being chased by his new best friend.

The next morning at breakfast Mrs. Chavez asked Henry what kind of dog he wants. "I'm warming up to the idea. I think the house could use a bit of joy, and a dog might be just the thing we need," Mrs. Chavez said happily.

Meanwhile, at Old Timer Rescue, Gladys, Phyllis, and Trudy were having breakfast. "Sisters, what should we do today?" Trudy asked. "Maybe we could go for a walk!" Gladys replied.
"We can't, guys; it's adoption day again, but I'm not going to get excited. I don't want to get my hopes up...again," Phyllis sadly stated.

Phyllis

Gladys

Trudy

All the senior dogs lined up and howled happily as new families walked in. Nobody stopped by Gladys, Phyllis, and Trudy. The sisters comforted each other and as Gladys kissed her sisters she said, "It will happen some-day...don't worry, guys."

Right before adoption day was over, Mrs. Chavez and Henry walked in. Henry beamed with excitement. "Mom, look at all the amazing dogs!" he shouted. "They are all so cute, how will I ever choose just one?" he wondered aloud.

Mrs. Chavez found a volunteer while Henry played with the dogs, "Sir, can you tell me which dog has been here the longest and which one may not have the best chances of being adopted?" The volunteer nodded and brought Mrs. Chavez over to Gladys, Phyllis, and Trudy.

"These girls have been here quite some time. Gladys is great. She's eight years old, and I'm not sure why someone hasn't picked her. Phyllis is nine years old. She's shy and keeps to herself, but once she knows you, she can be the sweetest dog. Trudy is the oldest at ten years old and is a snugglebug," the volunteer explained.

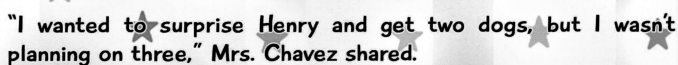

"I wanted to surprise Henry and get two dogs, but I wasn't planning on three," Mrs. Chavez shared.
"I understand," said the volunteer. "It's just that these three girls are bonded, and we would love for them to find a home together."

Old
Timer
Rescue

"Three dogs!" Mrs. Chavez thought nervously. "How would I care for three dogs and Henry?" Mrs. Chavez made her way over to the girls' area. She sat down slowly and smiled at the trio.

"Hello Gladys, Phyllis, and Trudy...how are you doggies doing?" Mrs. Chavez asked. Gladys jumped up with a pep in her step and immediately sat in Mrs. Chavez' lap. Trudy followed with a lick and a paw on her hand. Phyllis popped up her head, too afraid to move, and just stared at Mrs. Chavez.

"It's okay little one...you're safe, and I promise that I'm nice!" Mrs. Chavez said lovingly. Henry sat down next to his mom giggling with excitement. Gladys and Trudy playfully jumped on Henry and covered him with kisses, while Phyllis gradually made her way over to him and laid at his feet.

"Mom, they are all so sweet...I don't know who to choose," Henry said with regret in his voice.

Mrs. Chavez put her hand on Henry's and said, "They are bonded and that means they would be sad without each other."

Henry thought for a second. "Like the way we are sad without Dad?" Henry asked.

"Exactly," Mrs. Chavez replied.

In that moment Mrs. Chavez knew what she wanted to do. "Henry, let's bring them into our family. We can never replace Dad, but we can give these senior pups a great life. Will you help me do that?" Mrs. Chavez asked.

Henry was over the moon. "THREE DOGS!" he thrillingly yelled out. "Of course, I'll help! They are my new best friends, and can they please all sleep with me? Pretty please?!?"
I'll think about it," Mrs. Chavez laughed.

The volunteer started to pack Gladys' harness and blanket.
Gladys jumped for joy.
"Oh my gosh guys...I'm being adopted!" Trudy and Phyllis ran up
to her and jumped on her giving her playful kisses.
"We are so happy for you, but does this mean we won't see you
again?" Phyllis asked as her eyes filled with tears.

Gladys suddenly realized that she might no longer see her sisters. With her head down, Gladys said softly, "I love you guys so much." "We love you too," her senior sisters replied.

Just when the girls thought they would have to say goodbye forever, Mrs. Chavez and little Henry took Phyllis and Trudy and placed them in their harnesses and attached their leashes. "C'mon girls, it's time for us all to go home!" Henry said excitedly.

"We are getting adopted too, Gladys!" Trudy howled.
"We get to stay together!" yipped Phyllis. The girls climbed into
the back seat of the car. Henry sat in the middle and made sure

"Everything is going to be okay now, guys," Henry said happily. "We lost Dad, and we will always miss him, but that doesn't mean we can't love again, because we can...right, Mom?"

"Right," Mrs. Chavez whispered.

The girls walked into their new home with a great big yard they couldn't wait to explore. "C'mon bubbies...you get to share my room!" Henry exclaimed.

"Bubbies?" Mrs. Chavez asked.

"Yes, these are my new 'buddy babies'...I'm going to call them my bubbies—my old bubbies!" Henry squealed.

"It's been a long day, my sweet girls. Get some rest, and we'll explore the neighborhood tomorrow. Good night, and welcome home!" Mrs. Chavez said as she kissed each girl lovingly. With that, they drifted off to sleep in their brand-new home with their brand-new family.

Find the star(s) on each page. They are a reminder that even though our loved ones may be gone they are still with us every day.